DIARY of Farty Philip

Philip Kingsley's Journal

by Kiri Birch

Birch Tree Publishing

Birch Tree Publishing
All rights reserved, no part of this book may be produced, scanned, or distributed in any printed or electronic form without permission
© Copyright Birch Tree Publishing 2017
Brought to you by the Publishers of Birch Tree Publishing
ISBN: 978-1-927558-47-8

Illustrated by chief artist Rizky Nugraha

Birch Tree Publishing

To my husband, whose farts inspired me to write this story.

With love, your Stinky Butt

Kiri A Birch

THE BEGINNING

There was once a boy called Farty Philip. Actually, his real name was Philip Kingsley, but he got the nickname Farty Philip at school, and it stuck.

Could you guess how Farty Philip got his name? Farty (as he was known to his friends) had THE WORST farts ever! They were loud, and so, so smelly. It was a common myth within the school playground that Farty could knock out an entire class of small kids with one of his classic farts.

Nobody realized what a smelly, vegetable fart could do. But, as for all good things coming to those who wait, there's time to find out.

Farty Philip has a lot of friends. Each one has a nickname, but this all spirals from the fact that Farty got his nickname, and they wanted one too. Philip only moved to this school a few months ago, but already his name was epic among the kids. Now, having built up his circle of friends, they all have names...Club- hand Collin, Loose legs Liam, Boggle-Eyed Ian, and lastly Nimble Nina.

Technically, Nimble Nina wasn't a part of the gang because she is a girl and girls don't belong in a boys group. But, she had her uses. Especially when the correct answer sheet for the math homework was sat on Mr. Harris' desk. It still amazed the boys (although three of the four wouldn't admit it) how Nimble Nina managed to sneak into the classroom, take the answer sheet, and sneak back out UNDETECTED, all whilst the teacher was writing a 'simple' math question on the board.

But, back to the important story. Farty Philip. He now made a point of eating the grossest smelling vegetables he could find in the school cafeteria. Which wasn't hard, when you looked at the cooking. And it was even easier to understand when you looked at the cooks.

Not many people like Cook Babbage, the lead Cook. Most of the kids thought she was smelly and mean and never made anything tasty. Farty thought she was a nice lady though. She always gave Farty as many vegetables as he wanted, which was helpful for his quest in life to make the smelliest farts ever.

Because she was always kind to Farty, he was the only one in the school who didn't call her by her nickname...Cook Cabbage. Even so, the food wasn;t the easiest to digest, even for Farty and his smelly mission.

Farty just had to do what he had to do, for the sake of keeping up his reputation for all things stinky. Every lunchtime, no matter what, he forced down his portion of stinkathon vegetables. He'd learned pretty quickly which ones made the best pong, but it didn't make it easier to eat it. "Why were vegetables even invented?" was always one of the main points of discussion with the gang every lunchtime. Farty knew the answer. To make boys stink!

So, Farty Philip. How did he get his name? It all started on his first day at his new school. He and his Mum had moved ten miles away from where they were living before but he had to move schools because his old one was too far away to walk to each morning. Anyhow, he was going to senior school the following year so it wasn't too much of a deal to have his final year somewhere different.

Farty's Mum got a new job, a promotion (she had said at the time). She had worked as a receptionist at a law firm. When working there, she had been headhunted by the most famous lawyer in town. He never lost a case! (Or so it said on his TV adverts). This new job meant that Mum earned loads more money, meaning that Farty could do whatever after school club he wanted, but it also meant (unknown to his Mum, at the time of accepting the job) that she would have to be available at all hours of the day, for many hours, to organise the most unusual things for the lawyer man.

Go to the cafe and buy a very complex sounding coffee (what is a mocha locha latte creamy froth coffee anyway!), endless typing of letters (he must have a lot of friends to tell all his business to) and always driving him to places (to the cinema, and everything).

Farty missed his Mum because she was working all the time, but she seemed happy enough. She usually joined the lawyer on all his adventures. She said she was having fun. Farty figured that being a famous lawyer was a good career choice because he wouldn't have to do his own cooking, cleaning or shopping, EVER. His Mum did it for him, instead.

Back to Farty's first day at school. Farty was excited to check out the much bigger and shinier looking school, but he was excited to be starting "ninja karate" straight after his first day.
His Mum had already arranged for him to be in that group after school. One thing that Farty had not been looking forward to, however, was having to stand up in front of the whole class and say something interesting about himself.

Farty, who didn't really consider himself cool, didn't know what to say! Mr.Tibbetts, his new teacher, had put him right on the spot to think of something interesting. Farty had known this moment was coming- why hadn't he planned this better?!. Farty stood up, walked up to the front of the class, and started his introduction;

"My name is Philip Kingsley. I am nine years old, soon to be ten. I just moved to Kippersgate last month. My favorite subject is...

PFFFFFFFFFFFFFFFFFFFFFFFFFFFFFFFF...

The nerves got the better of him. He wasn't much of a public speaker. As he got more nervous his bottom had started to jitter. He thought he could sneak out a silent, but deadly fart as he stood at the front of the classroom. However today, his first day of new school, he was not going to be so lucky. The fart was so loud it echoed around the room, bouncing off the model skeleton in the corner and making its bones rattle.

Farty didn't know what to do. So, he just smiled and hoped that nobody had noticed. Everyone had noticed! And what was worse, it looked like everybody (including Mr. Tibbetts) was CHOKING!!! The smell was unbearable! Everyone was closing their eyes as the fart was making them teary!

Just as Farty was about to run out of the classroom (and possibly not stop running until he was all the way home), a lanky boy with long legs stood up, right at the back of the class. This boy would later turn out to be Loose Legs Liam, but Farty hadn't known that very soon they two boys would be creating this name for him. Anyhow, just as Farty was planning his escape route, the boy started to clap! To clap, no less!

"Woohoo, congratulations to the new boy" and just as everyone started turning around in confusion, he shouted, half laughing "that was the BEST FART EVER! So stinky so loud so....Awesome!! I've been trying to do one like that for years."

And that is how Philip;
1. got his nickname
2. got his first friend at his new school...Loose Legs Liam

Because Liam had been so impressed with Farty's fart, it only took until lunchtime for most of the other kids in the class to introduce themselves to him.

The boys from Farty's class came up and patted him on the back. The girls whispered and smiled at him as he walked past them in the lunchroom. To be fair, Farty never understood why girls were weird like that, and always whispering, but he didn't get the sense that they were being mean, so he was cool with the giggles.

And it only took the afternoon of his first day to get known to the rest of his school. Here's how the afternoon went; School assembly happened on Monday afternoons at Elmwood Elementary.

School assembly consisted of all the kids at school squashing themselves into the otherwise huge P.E. Gym to listen to Mr. Fimm the Head teacher talk about boring things for twenty minutes. Although it was a bit cramped in the gym, the kids didn't mind because it was the best opportunity of the day to either

1. braid each other's hair (if you were a girl)
                OR
2. play jokes on one another (if you were a boy)

Unknown to any kid on this particular afternoon however, things weren't going to go as normal. It started off normal enough, with all the kids being led into the hall. Obviously Farty was just following along and copying Loose Legs Liam because he had no idea what he should be doing, but he figured out pretty quickly to check the seat before you sit down- just as he was in line, waiting to sit, he spotted two boys in from of him.

One of the boys placed a banana skin on the other boy's chair, and before you know it, the banana skin did its job perfectly and caused the second boy to slip right off his chair as he sat down!

So, safely sat in his chair and waiting for Mr. Grimm to start talking (it was actually Mr. Fimm, but of course he had to have a suitable nickname that the boys could use as code for when he was coming around the corner and put a stop to their mischief) Farty was relaxed and reliving his epic morning fart, daydreaming away.

The daydream was not destined to be finished. Just as Farty was getting to the juicy (i.e. farty) part of his daydream, an awful scream came from a girl just a few spaces forward from him. She jumped up in the air as if she had sat on a pin! He could see there was no pin or banana peel on her chair, so it couldn't be either of those things. It took only another second to notice the problem...a HUGE black spider on the back of the seat in front of the girls.

Farty wasn't quite close enough to see it properly, but he was pretty sure it was one of those spiders with hairy legs and more than likely big teeth. He wasn't afraid of spiders (because really, what boy is?!) but at that moment he was glad to be far enough away from it that it wouldn't jump on him. Which is unlike all of the girls around the first girl, who had now realised what the fuss was all about and were now oining in the shrieking and jumping up around on the chairs.

Now, Mr. Fimm was a strict head teacher who didn't like to be interrupted at all when he was telling all of the children the important news of the day. Why weren't they listening to his story about the dustbins being collected on a different day this week? To add to his bad mood, he was not impressed when a girl started to shriek and shout, something about a spider. Why are children afraid of spiders? He wondered. A little spider won't hurt any of them. Mr. Fimm could not tolerate the noisiness. He was getting more and more angry as the spider commotion got louder and louder.

Eventually, he gave a nice big shout to "SHUT UUUUUUUUPPPPPPP" in the microphone, just enough to scare the girl even more than she was scared by the spider....into utter silence! She just stood there, like a statue, obviously still in shock from the spider, with the added humiliation of being shouted at by the Grimm Fimm. All eyes were on her...or the huge spider.

So there Farty was, sat a few rows back from the stunned and terrified girl, wondering what was going to happen next?
He definitely didn't want to draw attention to himself from the Grimm Fimm by trying to help the girl. However, he knew he had to help somehow! The spider might come towards him. And then it came to him...when the room was still in shock from the shout down the microphone, he did what Farty does best...he let out a HUGE fart!!

And boy, his fartiness had definitely not wavered from this morning because the moment the fart hit his nostrils, he knew that extra portion of baked beans at lunchtime had done their job. The smell was horrendous!

In what seemed like a lifetime, the smell started to waft its way forward to the girl. Farty was hoping that the smell would bring her back to reality and hurry her up to sit down, but in reality it was even better than this. YES, everybody was choking and YES, it was bringing tears to his own eyes, but it was the best solution that Farty could have come up with at that moment.

And boy, it did its job! The moment the toxic fumes hit the girl's nostrils, she fainted! Right back into her chair. Even better than that, the spider got a waft and decided to take a run for its life- there was no way he was going to be hanging around those shadows of the cool chairs in the gym any more- something ridiculously smelly was invading his new home!

So off the spider shot, straight for the door, deciding (rather prematurely in his opinion, but the decision had been forced under duress) that it was time to build a web across the history teachers office door instead of staying in the gym, where clearly it was not safe from toxic fumes any more.

Now, in the three minutes that this whole saga happened, Mr. Grimm had gotten very irate with all the children. How dare they keep interrupting him! The cheek of it! But, at least the girl had come to her senses and sat back down.

Unfortunately, what Mr. Grimm didn't realise, is that yes, the girl had sat down, but most of the children in the middle of the room appeared to now have succumb to a bad cough. Of course, if good old Grimm had been more attentive, he would have realised the kids were all being gassed by Farty's epic solution to the spider dilemma. But no, he had his assembly to talk through and that is what he was going to do!

Loose Legs Liam and Farty went to the 'ninja karate' after school club that evening. Farty was still on a high from being so popular at school already, but what really made his day is how clumsy Liam was. It is easy to guess how Liam then got his nickname- try as he might, he had the coordination of a hippopotamus trying to do ballet. He ended up on his back with every move, even doing a karate chop with his hand!

In fairness to Liam, Farty wasn't that good either, but they had a great time with some male bonding during the karate class. There's nothing quite like laughing at each other to seal a friendship. At the end, whilst waiting for the Mums to pick them up, they came up with the nickname 'loose legs Liam'

Farty gave his Mum the lowdown of how the day had gone and despite being utterly disgusted that her beautiful son could be so vile and embarrass her by farting out loud to the whole class, she was super pleased that he was getting on well in his new school.

Farty didn't really understand how his Mum could be embarrassed that he had farted, but he was secretly glad that she wasn't worried about him. He didn't like to stress her out, especially because she was new to her job. Both of them knew what it was like starting somewhere new.

So... that wraps up how Farty got on during his first day of school, and how he got the name Farty. Little did he know of all the adventures he would be having with his friends as he went to bed that night.

Farty Philip's Valentine

Now, Farty isn't what you consider a romantic kind of kid. He likes girls and all, but only the ones that could impress him with their tree climbing skills or epic karate chops. Apart from that, he found them kind of boring. Apart from Nimble Nina, Farty had found that some girls, especially the older ones at school, weren't impressed with loud and amazingly stinky farts.

Their problem though, not his. He was cool with his classmates. What Farty had noticed recently was that his Mum was weirder than normal. She was looking at her phone and giggling at the messages. Farty didn't even know that anyone text his Mum, apart from him. And it couldn't be his messages that she was looking at because he was sat in the same room as her when the messages came in.
It was all very peculiar.

It wasn't just the messages. Oh no. His Mum had started taking longer in the bathroom as well, when she was getting ready for work. She would sing and hum to herself (or what was supposed to be herself, except Farty could hear every word through his bedroom wall because it was next to the bathroom).

Her singing wasn't the best but it was better than his, so he didn't say anything. The only annoying thing about her taking so long in the bathroom is that Farty's 'getting ready for school in 3 minutes' had to be adjusted to 'getting ready in ten seconds' because his Mum was taking up the bathroom much longer than usual.

Now, Farty was epic at getting ready in super quick time, but even for him, ten seconds was pushing it. The other day it took him the whole walk into school before he realised he had toothpaste all over his face. And who knows how many times he had forgotten his school tie, or to put socks on this past month.

One morning about a week ago, his Mum had asked him how she looked. To Farty, she looked exactly the same as normal, except she looked like she had lipstick on. This wasn't the first time that he'd seen her in lipstick, but this lipstick wasn't the same as normal.

It was bright red. Farty didn't have the heart to tell his Mum that she looked like an exotic fish (you know, the kind that you see at the aquarium that looked like they could suction to the glass with their big lips). He said she looked great (what does a little white lie hurt, to your Mum?).

His Mum blushed and told him that he was the best son ever. She even gave him a big wet kiss on the head. Farty thought that was kind of gross but figured he would let his Mum act strange for a while. Better for her to be a gushy happy mood, than a bad one.

One evening when they were having dinner, Farty's Mum asked him what his plans were for Valentines Day. Apparently it was on Saturday coming up. He explained that apart from the obvious football club on Saturday morning, and going to get a milkshake and maybe go to the cinema with his mates in the afternoon, he didn't have any plans.

What other plans would you have on a Saturday?

His Mum had asked him if he was going to be around as there was someone she would like him to meet. This didn't bother Farty at all, but he was curious. Maybe this person was the reason for the fish lipstick?

Mum said it was a guy, who according to her was her new boyfriend. In honesty, the first thing that went through Farty's mind when she said that was 'my mum is way too old for a boyfriend!' and nearly as quickly he thought 'ewwwww, my Mum has been kissing a guy'. He didn't share these thoughts with his Mum. He'd been allowed to stay up really late the last few days which Farty could only put down to his Mums good mood, so he didn't want to ruin his winning streak of ice cream before dinner and bed at midnight.

His Mum asked him if he would mind to help cook some food on Saturday night for when the 'boyfriend' came over. His name was Howard. His Mum specially requested Farty's help with his famous spaghetti bolognese. In return for his help in the kitchen, Farty would be allowed to pick whatever desert he wanted for the three of them. Sweeeeeeeet! They would go shopping for the food on the Saturday afternoon.

Meeting Howard was cool. Farty's first thoughts about him were;
1. Whoah, he is tall.
2. He has big muscles. He must be mega-strong.
3. His beard is impressive. He wondered how many chocolate bars he could hide in it, for emergency purposes.

Howard introduced himself and asked Farty some questions. Thankfully, it turned out that they liked the same things- karate and football, among other things. Howard worked at an office in the city quite close to the football grounds. From his office (so he said) he can see all the matches being played. It was better than being in the best seats of the stadium. And even better, it was free! The best bit of this story was that Howard had said that he would take Farty to his office one day soon that he could come and see for himself. Nice one!

The spag bol went off without a hitch. Everyone loved it, and Howard was impressed that Farty knew how to cook it with barely any help from his Mum. Nobody noticed that he'd forgotten to put in the onions. He didn't think they noticed that he put in a bit too much garlic, until Howard laughed at something and both Farty and his Mum recoiled at the smell of his breath. Howard was very embarrassed and apologized profusely until it was noticed by him that both Farty and his Mums breath was just as bad! Farty's Mum joked and said that it made a nice change that it was Fartys breath that smelt, and not his butt.

For dessert, Farty had picked his favourite chocolate brownie. It also happened to be his Mums favourite too. Everything was going well with the dessert, until the minor hiccup of Howard choking on the first bite of brownie! Farty knew what to do in this situation, it had happened to him before when he took a bite far bigger than his mouth could handle. Before his Mum even realised what was going on, Farty ran over behind Howard, placed his hands around his back (so it looked like he was cuddling Howard from behind), and squeezed really hard!

Even though it actually didn't happen in slow motion, for a few seconds it looked like it was slow mo- the piece of chocolate brownie came flying out of Howards mouth and landed right on Farty's Mums plate. And so his Mums face changed into a series of different emotions in the space of five seconds; bewildered as to how a piece of squidgy chocolate brownie had flown out of nowhere and found itself splattered to her plate; terrified when she realized that the brownie had just evacuated itself from Howard throat as seconds before it had been choking him.

Baffled as to how said squidgy chocolate brownie had managed to evacuate itself by Howard having done nothing to make that happen; grossed out by the chocolate brownie squidged to her plate; horrified that Howard had nearly basically passed out in front of her (death by choking is a real thing); and finally, totally amazed that Farty had accomplished a life-saving emergency procedure right in front of her eyes and she hadn't even finished her mouthful of food! The only give away that Farty had saved Howard in super quick time (apart from the obvious flying chocolate squidgy brownie) was that as Farty had used all his energy to squeezed Howard's chest, he'd accidentally squeezed his own butt cheeks... and..."Brrrrrrrrrrrrrrrrrrrpppppppppppppp" OUT SLIPPED A MASSIVE FART!

After the initial shock of the experience had passed, all three of them actually all had a little laugh about it. It was kind of funny to see a grown-up choke like that! Because his Mum was so excited that Howard hadn't passed out there and then, she totally forgot to tell Farty off for his epic guff just as he had saved the day. In a way, this was too bad because Farty was actually very impressed with duration, smell and noise that the fart had made. Maybe emergency situations make farts all round better in every way?! Still, Farty figured it was safer not to bring the fart up with his Mum again. She was generally not as impressed with his farts as he was.

Just as his Mum got up from the dinner table to make a drink for all three of them, Howard quickly put his hand under the table to Farty "give me high five, buddy?" Initially Farty was confused, but he figured that Howard was referring to him saving his life.

But no...Farty nearly fell off his chair when Howard spoke again. "That was an EPIC FART you did earlier man...I can't wait to hear your tips on how to do them like that! I've never been able to do them like that!". Howard was jealous of Fartys FARTS! He was really beginning to like this fella!

After dinner, Farty and his Mum cleaned up the plates and then they sat in the lounge for a bit. Because the adults were mostly just talking adult (i.e. boring) stuff, Farty soon gave up and said he was going to his room to bed. He'd had a cool night with Howard and his Mum, but adults talking about the weather was nearly as boring to Farty as watching the news. Dull. Dull. Dull.

Howard shook his hand and said good night, and promised Farty that they would arrange their football date soon. As he was lying in bed, Farty could hear his Mum giggling and having a great old time.
Who even knows what adults have to laugh about? Adults have to go out to work all day, every day, pay bills and do grocery shopping... what could possibly be funny in their lives?

Farty must have fallen asleep for a bit because the next thing he heard was Howard in the hallway, getting ready to leave. Farty crept out of his room, just to see what was happening. Big mistake! Big, big, BIG MISTAKE!

Just as he made it to the top of the stairs, he spotted the scene he couldn't forget for a while... his Mum and Howard kissing!! It was so gross. He made a mental note to never creep out and look at what the adults were doing ever again! Hopefully the image of his Mum kissing Howard wouldn't be burned into his mind forever.

He hoped he could get back to sleep again and not have nightmares about it. Kissing was so...nasty! All that spit. Only a dog would ever be allowed to lick Farty's face like that. Never EVER A GIRL.

Farty Philip at the zoo

Farty was getting ready to go to the zoo. His Mum had been really busy with work lately, so she had said for a treat, they would spend the day at the zoo together. Both Farty and his Mum loved the zoo, and it was always the place they would pick to go together to have a 'Mummy/son date'. Although in fairness, Farty didn't tell his mates that he was going on a date with his Mum. That was something he preferred to keep between him and his Mum.

Farty was a 'lions and tigers' kind a boy. His Mum said that he liked all the strong animals because he was super strong like them; a protector. This was quite true, Farty did want to protect his Mum. He knew that she was good at looking after herself, but a boy's role is to make sure that his Mum is OK: everyone knows that.

His Mums favourite animals were the exotic birds. You know, like the Green Amazon parrots and African Greys. His Mum always said that she wanted to have a pet parrot, but she didn't think it was cool to keep them in a cage. That, and she also said that they smell really bad if you don't clean them out regularly enough.

That's why she loved coming to the zoo: it's like the birds lived in their natural habitat all of the time, and it was somebody else's job to clean up their poop. So, with his safari hat and binoculars at the ready they headed to the zoo.

On the way to the zoo, Farty and his Mum stocked up on their donuts and coffee. Donuts and coffee were for dates only. Obviously Farty didn't have coffee ('juice of the devil' he called it) but he had a huge blue slushy instead. They had to keep up their energy for the zoo because it was a huge place.

When they got there the queue wasn't too big, which was great. They had been at the zoo before when they had to wait half an hour in a queue. That sucked because it was all time wasted that they could be inside looking around. But today, they got lucky.
Before they went off to see any of the animals, they looked at the feeding schedule. The feeding schedule informed the visitors when each animal was being fed, so that they can go and watch it.
It was kind of a lunchtime show. Of course, they had to go and see the tigers eating their lunch at 11am.

Farty had seen it all before, but he never got bored of it: he imagined where the zoo keepers had got all the meat from. It's not like you could go the supermarket and buy enough meat for a tiger. His Mum had said years ago that the meat was the zookeepers that hadn't arrived at work on time.

Farty had laughed it off at the time thinking this was a joke, but as he got older he had thought about it more and more. He was thinking, you never hear of zookeepers that turn up to work late and live to tell the tale... maybe his Mum was right. He didn't want to know: that would be creepy if it was true! So, the origin of the feeding meat was still one of life's unanswered mysteries.

After the feeding of the tigers, there was a break from the feeding until 1pm when the birds would be fed. Farty's Mum always loved this: if you got there early and queued for a little while, the bird handler would give some food out that you could hold it in your hand.
Then the parrots would fly around your head, spot that you have food and come and sit on your arm to eat it.

Personally, Farty wasn't too chuffed with the idea of a bird with a beak the size of his head coming to eat lunch on his arm his Mum said that birds only eat fruit and vegetation, but hey, Farty's arm could look similar to a bean sprout if the bird was colour blind.

Either way, it was cool to watch the birds fly around and Farty knew that his Mum loved the birds sitting on her. His Mum always joked that she looked like a female pirate when Roger, the huge Macaw parrot, sat on her arm. Roger was her favourite.

They headed off to look first in the Reptile House. They saw a few snakes of varying length and width (and different level of danger from venom, too), turtles (or tortoise, Farty could never tell which was which) some spiky lizards and best of all, crocodiles! Of course the crocodiles were sleeping because they always were, but still, they were really cool to look at. And, they were huge! Farty was sure that he saw one crocodile wink and smile at him (probably because the crocodile would very much enjoy eating him) but his Mum said that was just his imagination.

Farty reckoned that the crocodiles were just pretending to sleep, waiting for their opportunity to pounce on the tastiest looking passer-by. Good job there was glass between them both.
They headed up into the 'big animal' region and had a walk around to see the zebras, camels, the lone rhinoceros and the two big elephants. Farty's Mum liked the elephants.

They both got to the tiger den with ten minutes to spare before feeding time. Unfortunately, even though they were early there was already a crowd three people deep looking through the glass, right where the male and female tiger were sunbathing. Farty reckoned it must be a coach tour of old foreign people because he couldn't understand a word they were saying. Farty's Mum could see a little if she stood on tiptoes, but there was no way that Farty was ever going to get a look in with all the people around.

This was a highly frustrating situation for Farty he couldn't even use his binoculars to see the tigers if people were blocking his view. His Mum suggested that they come back a bit later and he was just about to give in and agree, when he had a cunning plan he told his Mum to stay still in her place in the crowd, he'd be back in two minutes.

Then he squirmed and struggled his way through the crowd (good job they were mostly adults, they couldn't tell who was pushing them in the legs because Farty was too low and quick to see) right into the deepest depths of where all the people were accumulated, and... PSSSSSSSSSSSSSSSSSSSSSSSSSSSSSSSSSSSSTTTT!

He let out an almighty 'silent, but deadly' guff.

Farty had a noisy one stored up and he knew that he could use it if needed, but he didn't want the holiday makers to realise that it was him. Better if they blamed one another for ruining their tiger feeding experience.

The ninja fart (named so by Farty because it had stealth and power, but was invisible to the naked eye) took a couple of minutes to rise, but boy oh boy, when it did, it had the perfect effect on the holiday makers!

They looked around, bewildered at one another, trying to figure out (and presumably asking one another in their weird language) who had dropped that stink bomb.

It didn't take long for people to start holding their noses and hand signalling to one another to say that they were moving.

Fresh air was needed by all, and they started moving back towards the open air, away from one another quite fast! One lady looked like somebody was waving a pair of stinky old socks in her face.
She looked very unhappy! Rather unfortunately (for her) she also appeared to be gagging, but nothing was coming out. "Too bad for the tourists" thought Farty, but hey, when you've got to fart, you might as well put it to good use!

Now, Farty and his Mum could see the tigers! Farty stood in the middle of the crowd for one more minute before he could see his Mum, who looked very stunned that everybody but her had suddenly decided that tiger watching was not their interest any more.
She asked if Farty knew why they had all left, to which (of course) he said he had no idea!

Thankfully, his Mum believed him. The smell of the fart has dissipated sufficiently that his Mums nose was used to the underlying whiff of stench that she couldn't detect in an outdoor environment. The ninja fart was well worth it. The tiger feeding show was epic!

The zookeeper was surprised to see that where there was a crowd of at least one hundred people just a few minutes before, there was now only a little boy and his Mum. Even so, they seemed to enjoy it. The tigers were on top form today, showing off their big teeth and rumbling growls.

After a slice of pizza each for lunch, Farty and his Mum headed to the bird sanctuary. Fartys Mum was having a great time and he knew that she was happy. She was saying at lunch how great everything had gone so far today; firstly, no queue at the front of the zoo; getting to see all of the animals in the reptile house; saying hello to the big animals; and to top it off (!!!) NOBODY else watching the tiger feeding show. "You can't pay to get such a good view," She kept saying. Farty was secretly hoping that the bird show went off without a hitch, to make it a very satisfying zoo day for them both.

As they headed up to the bird sanctuary, Farty spotted a couple of the adult tourists that had been at the feeding show just a little while earlier. The tourists looked and smiled at Farty and his Mum. Clearly, none of them had figured out it was Farty who was to blame for their missing of the show!

Farty and his Mum got to the bird sanctuary and (as normal) took a seat at the back. The back seats were the best seats in the aviary because the seats got gradually higher facing up from the stage, so that meant that the birds would see them first as they flew upwards. Thankfully, not too many people were in the seats so Farty thought that were safe. Until...2 minutes before the bird show began, in came the HUGE crowd of tourists again!

They must have spotted that Farty and his Mum were coming into the aviary and thought they were good people to follow! There was no way that his Mum would get any bird feed now, not with so many people blocking the way between the stage and where they were sat.
What could he do?!

As quick as he thought that there was nothing he could do, it came to him! Farty was impressed by his quick thinking...he would drop a ninja fart again, to get everyone to clear out. With best results, the tourists would leave (and maybe Farty and his Mum would be the only ones for the show again, or at the very least the tourists would move seats so that they weren't between Farty, his Mum and the stage).

Farty excused himself from his Mum (just so she wouldn't figure out what he was doing) and said that he was going to the toilet. He got to the steps in the middle of all the seats, bent down to pretend he was doing up his shoelace, and got ready to once again drop his silent ninja stink bomb. One...two...three... BRRRRRRRRRRRRRRPPPPPPPPPPPPP PPPPPPPPP. THAT WAS NOT A SILENT ONE!

For a second, Farty didn't know what to do. There was no way he could look up to see if anyone had noticed. He knew straight away that one hundred pairs of eyes would be on him...there was no way they could have missed it. The aviary was designed so that everybody could hear the bird keeper talking when there was a huge crowd.

There was also microphones and speakers placed all around the room! Unfortunately this meant that Farty's epic bomb just ricocheted around the building, making it sound ten times louder and more echoed than it was normally. Even normally, it was LOUD! In the aviary, it was DEAFENING!

Although he knew this was a bad situation (who wants 100 people blaming him for an epic smelly fart) what Farty feared the most was his Mum! He definitely did not want to get eye contact from her right now. Who knows what she would say or do! Whatever it was, it wasn't going to be good.

So there he was crouched down on the floor, pretending to do up his shoelaces, thinking how on earth he was going to get away with this one, when...apparently out of nowhere, came a loud screech.

"Smelly bum…smelly bum…smelly bum". Farty was thinking (still crouched down)…it wasn't one of the trainers, it was too screechy for that. It wasn't his Mum, there's no way that she would say that in front of all those people. He figured it out…it was Roger the Macaw! What an awesome parrot he was!

Roger flew right up to Farty and landed right on his head. He started singing his song again "smelly bum…smelly bum…smelly bum". DEFINITELY no way he was getting away with it now. Although he knew there was no getting away with it anyway.

Not only did he have everyone staring at him, Farty now had a huge parrot with an even larger beak on his head. Oh, how Farty was worried for his bean sprout arms! Farty attempted to straighten up with his arms nicely tucked in at his side, but he didn't get very far at all. Every time he moved his head, Roger dug his claws in. Apparently Farty's head did not make a good perch for a parrot to rest.

Thankfully the trainer came to rescue him quickly (not that it felt like it to Farty). The bird zookeeper came casually walking down the steps to where Farty still crouched down (not that Farty could see that she was coming) and said in a calm voice "And that, ladies and gentlemen, will demonstrate to you that Roger the Macaw is very familiar with potent odours in the aviary". The crowd roared with laughter.

The bird keeper went on to say "fortunately it is not me who make these odours, but one of my colleagues who unfortunately is not here today to see this spectacle. If he had been here, he would be very proud of Rogers keen sense of smell". And again, the whole crowd laughed to the point of having tears in their eyes.

"To say thank you to this fine young gentleman for opening the show, he and his mother are welcome to look after Roger for the rest of the show. Perhaps not on the boys head! Turning to Farty's Mum, the trainer asked "Mum, would you be as kind as to take Roger off your sons head. I believe Roger will quite happily sit on your arm, if you wish".

And that is how Farty was saved from his mother's wrath. Not only did he get a standing ovation from the crowd for his epic farty show opening, his Mum appeared to totally forget the embarrassment of the whole situation as soon as she had Roger sat on her arm.

Roger the parrot was as good as gold and he sat on Farty's Mums arm for the entire show. Farty wasn't wholly convinced that Roger wasn't eyeing up his arms for a good gnaw, but he thought better then to bring it up with his Mum. After all, Farty was the reason that Roger had obliged himself to sharing his company with the two of them.

Farty's Mum didn't mention the 'big bang' fart. Except once in the car on the way home. She muttered something to herself as she drove past the café that they'd had a donut in for breakfast. Farty could have sworn she said "no more donuts for now, they make your guts rotten".

Farty gets sick

This week hadn't been a fantastic one as far as Farty was concerned. He'd actually been poorly for quite a lot of it. Farty's sickness started back on Saturday. Now, Saturday is never really a good day to get sick on because it means that you are not allowed to do anything fun with the weekend. You're not allowed (or able) to go out with friends or really do anything at all unless it involves being in bed. And nothing fun ever happens in bed.

Farty hadn't been able to go to the skate park. He didn't mind too much. He had epic skateboard skills (or so he thought) so one week wouldn't kill him to miss. However, he was disappointed when his Mum told him he wasn't allowed out in the afternoon for a burger.
His Mum had done the kind thing and brought him a burger, but he just couldn't stomach it.

And you know things are bad when Farty doesn't want to eat his burger and fries! His Mum had immediately known that Farty was sick when he'd refused his burger, and sent him straight to bed, to rest. Farty didn't even have it in him to argue.

Now. I hear you were asking what had mysteriously come over Farty to make him so green at the gills? That is a good question! It had all started a few evenings before on Wednesday night, when Farty was invited to his friend's house. It was Club- hand Collins place, but Loose legs Liam and Boggle Eyed Ian had also come for a sleepover.

Nimble Nina had been invited, but she turned down the offer to 'suffocate half to death in a room full of stinky boy's to watch a girly film with her Mum and sisters. She knew how bad those boys smelled so she knew to steer clear of them.

The evening started off pretty well. Farty's Mum was going out on a date night with Howard so Farty was asked to be responsible and make sure they don't get up to too much trouble whilst she's gone. In exchange for this, he was allowed to go straight to Club Hand's house after school. Farty did what he was told (he didn't want to face the wrath of his mother once he got home the next day).

The boys played out by the park on the way home from school, but left there after a group of toddlers came by with their parents. Toddlers were a pest when they come to the park you have to let them go on everything first because they're small and that's what you're supposed to do.

Or at least that's what their Mums had said. This made everything in the park 100% slower. The other annoying thing about toddlers is that they're just not good at sharing. The boys would move out of the way of the slide and let the toddlers play there and before you know it, the little terrors were following them to the swings.

They moved out of the way of the swings and they were followed to the roundabout. You can't cause any mischief with a group of 2 year olds running around after you! So the boys quickly gave up on the park. They started to head back to Club Hand's house to attempt to continue building the tree house that all four boys had started making the summer before. Technically it wasn't a treehouse yet.

More like a platform floor. And by platform floor, what is actually meant is one plank of wood that Club Hands Dad had thrown into the tree and surprisingly it had landed in a somewhat horizontal position among the strong branches. It was a good start but as yet none of the boys had managed to actually climb up the tree far enough to get to the plank of wood. Today's project was to build some steps up the tree house.

The boys hunted around on the way back from the park for anything that could resemble a step. Surprisingly, there weren't any rope ladders lying around that route, so they ended up with the best they could; find two relatively sturdy branches, a few rocks and an old bit of strong rope.

Club Hands Dad had immediately told them that this was not going to be sufficient to take a step ladder, and that he would help Club Hands that weekend to make something more sufficient. With that in mind, the boys attempted to climb the tree unaided by the rope ladder for about half an hour, before they realized for the (possibly) one millionth time that they were not going to be able to climb it.

It was after the snack that Club Hands Mum made the boys that things got exciting. But, we'll come to that in a minute. Club Hands Mums snack deserves a mention. Hot dog fingers! Club Hands Mum was cool, she liked to decorate food to make it look spooky or gory or funny.

Today she had gone for the creepy look hot dogs with a small slice cut out of the top of the sausage, to make it look like a real finger. When you put the ketchup on it, they looked awesome! So...the bit where things get messy. The boys were discussing (over their creepy fingers snack) who is the smelliest one of them all?

Now, we're not talking 'I didn't have a shower this morning' smelly, or 'I've been wearing the same socks for four days' smelly (although Boggle Eyed Ian admitted this was him, but the boys already knew this from nearly being knocked out when he took off his shoes earlier) they were discussing FARTING.

To be honest, the boys already knew who the winner of the competition was because Farty was always the one with the stickiest farts, but it never hurt to keep re-checking because one of these days, surely one of the other boys will win, maybe just once.

Anyhow, that discussion soon evolved into what was going to be the turning point for Farty's stomach for the rest of the week.
What concoction could the boys make to see who could get the stinkiest, greenest guffs? Obviously the boys knew the standard; cabbage, brussel sprouts and baked beans. But they had to try something bigger and better this time, if they were ever going to win the stinkiest fart challenge.

The boys rooted around Club Hands kitchen cupboards (his Mum didn't mind) and found the following; Cauliflower Lots of cheese (all different flavours) Bok choy (the boys had no idea what this actually was, Club Hands Mum told them the name. All they knew is that it was green, kind of looked like a cabbage and Club Hands Mum had said that it "can make you slightly gassier than normal")

None of the boys really knew how to cook much (apart from Farty, who had his specialty dishes) so they asked Club Hands Mum to cook some food with that. She came up with the best meal ever- cauliflower cheese with a side order of bok choy. She also found some brussel sprouts as an added bonus side order.

The food was delicious. Each boy ate as much as they possibly could, to ensure that they were going to have the best farts for later that night. Farty's stomach started to rumble about an hour after dinner, but he was used to this- the best farts take effort on your guts. What he wasn't expecting was the stomach growling all night long! Even when the boys were heading to bed, his belly was really starting to grumble. It sounded like a monster was growling from inside him!

The boys headed to bed to set their cunning plan into action get in the bedroom, get comfortable, and see what stinkiness follows. For perhaps the first time in Farty's life, he actually didn't want to risk farting. Obviously he knew that he would have the smelliest farts (because he always did) but what with his stomach churning over and over, he just couldn't be sure that something else might come out of his bottom if he let one rip.

Before too long, the boys were cracking out some epic stinkers. That bok choy had really worked!! The best ones were eye watering! The worst ones were just 'mildly insulting' (as Club Hands Mum had out it). They certainly were impressive, choking farts that night. Still, Farty could tell that things weren't right.

He felt kinda sick, especially when smelling all the farts. This was definitely not normal. He was normally the best at distinguishing individual fart ingredients, but he couldn't even get a waft of anyone's fart without wanting to be sick!

School was torturous the next morning for Farty. For a very unusual change, even his own farts were making his stomach churn. He had to go home by lunchtime because he really couldn't be sure whether he was actually going to be sick or poop himself as he needed to let one go.

The girls in the class were generally disgusted by the smells Farty normally made, but they wouldn't come near him that day.
Mr. Tibbetts had asked Farty why his face was looking so green.
All Farty could whisper, was "my bum". Then he got told off by Mr. Tibbetts for saying 'bum'. He couldn't win!

By the time Farty got home just after lunch, he was well and truly ready to be making friends with the toilet. Nobody wants to know what happened in the toilet that day, but it was NASTY! Even Farty's Mum was worried about him. It wasn't like Farty to be sat on a toilet for three hours!

By Friday things were BAD!!! Farty couldn't fart as he wanted to because he still wasn't sure if anything liquid might follow the fart out of his bottom. Farty's Mum rang the Doctor. It was so unlike Farty to be in bed all day!

Whilst his Mum waited outside the bedroom, the Doctor gave Farty the 'once over'. He checked his breathing, his arms and legs, listened to his heart, and then he went outside to speak to his Mum.

"I'm afraid it's bad news" Doctor Jenkins told Farty's Mum. "Bad news indeed". Farty's Mum was getting really worried now. "What is the problem Doctor" she asked "Is he really sick?"

Dr. Jenkins pulled a sad and worried face "Oh yes, it is bad". "He is very sick"

"I have never smelt anything quite like what that boy is coming out within there. I believe his guts have well and truly taken a beating. I would say....cauliflower with a hint of brussel sprouts. Serious stuff. He is going to be smelling like that for a good few days yet, I'll say.

No vegetables for him for at least a week. Not unless you want him to smell that way for the rest of the month"
Well, you can imagine Farty's Mums surprise when she heard that! No vegetables for a week. What a lovely change that would make! Perhaps her house might not smell like Farty's fart for a few days!

Farty's Mum went in to Farty the good news he'd eaten some rotten vegetables (possible the brussel sprouts that Club Hands Mum had been trying to get someone to eat from the other day) and it had made only him sick because he had insisted on eating a great deal.
"That will teach you for always trying to be the smelliest boy in class" she said. "You well and truly got your wish granted this time".

Farty was relieved but he could only make out half a laugh- he didn't want any poop accidents happening in his bed. He promised his Mum that he wouldn't eat that many vegetables in one sitting again. Farty's Mum may have accidentally forgotten to mention that Dr. Jenkins hadn't recommended vegetables for the rest of the week: no point making the boy suffer any more than he needed to.

You will be glad to know that apart from one boring and long weekend of lying in bed with a tummy ache, Farty made a full recovery. WELL...full recovery except that he was wary of his veggies for a few days after the event. But, even Farty knew he had a reputation to keep up.

The first few times that he let one rip at school the next week, he had to be careful and make doubly sure that it was just guff (and nothing liquid) coming out of his bottom. And after he knew that he was in the 'safe zone' with his farting, he was all better. Club Hand Collin didn't keep up his 'smelliest fart' award for long!

The End

Stay tuned for Book Two

www.ingramcontent.com/pod-product-compliance
Lightning Source LLC
Chambersburg PA
CBHW071643040426
42452CB00009B/1740